50¢
OR

FUN FACTS ABOUT
Farm History

Written by
Ray H. Miller

Illustrated by
Andrew Crabtree

The ERTL Company, Inc. would like to thank the following companies, individuals, and organizations, who helped make Fun Facts About Farm History possible:

AGCO Corporation; Alfa Laval Agri; CF MotorFreight; Corel Corporation; Deere & Company; Farm Safety 4 Just Kids; Jody Norman of Florida Archives; B.W. Hoffmann; Steve Davis of Living History Farms, Des Moines, Iowa; NASA; Lorna Trowbridge of The Old Farmer's Almanac; New Holland North America, Inc.; and Stan Harris of the U.S. Department of Agriculture

PHOTO CREDITS

AGCO CORPORATION
Page 15 photo of Model 4660 courtesy of AGCO Corp.

ALFA LAVAL AGRI
Page 9 photo of dairy barn interior courtesy of Alfa Laval Agri.

CF MOTORFREIGHT
Page 25 photo of truck courtesy of CF MotorFreight.

COREL PROFESSIONAL PHOTOS
Cover photo of barn courtesy of Corel Corp.
Page 5 photo of barn courtesy of Corel Corp.
Page 13 photo of barn courtesy of Corel Corp.
Page 17 photo of farm courtesy of Corel Corp.
Page 21 photo of barn courtesy of Corel Corp.

FLORIDA ARCHIVES
Page 7 inset photo of harvesting courtesy of Florida Archives.
Page 11 inset photo of Bull Gas Tractor courtesy of Florida Archives.
Page 13 inset photo of cattle courtesy of Florida Archives.
Page 19 inset photo of John Deere Tractor courtesy of Florida Archives.

B.W. HOFFMANN
Page 23 photo of supermarket courtesy of B.W. Hoffman.

JOHN DEERE
Cover photo of Model 8760 courtesy of Deere & Company.
Page 7 photo of Model 8960 courtesy of Deere & Company.

LIVING HISTORY FARMS
Page 15 inset photo of horse and plow courtesy of Living History Farms.
Page 17 inset photo of pigs courtesy of Living History Farms.
Page 21 inset photo of woman in farmhouse courtesy of Living History Farms.

NASA
Page 29 photo of scientist and plants courtesy of NASA.
Page 29 inset photo of hydroponic lettuce courtesy of NASA.

NEW HOLLAND NORTH AMERICA, INC.
Page 11 photo of TR™97 Combine courtesy of New Holland North America, Inc.

THE OLD FARMER'S ALMANAC
Page 27 inset photo of 1883 almanac courtesy of The Old Farmer's Almanac.
Page 27 photo of 1995 almanac appears with the permission of The Old Farmer's Almanac.

U.S. DEPARTMENT OF AGRICULTURE
Page 9 inset photo of dairy cows courtesy of U.S.D.A.
Page 23 inset photo of general store courtesy of U.S.D.A.
Page 25 inset photo of train courtesy of U.S.D.A.

Printed in the U.S.A.
ISBN 1-887327-03-7

TABLE OF CONTENTS

DOWN ON THE FARM

Fun Facts About Farm History will show you a side of farm history you've never seen. This book takes an extraordinary look at how farms and farming have changed over the years. Whether it's an 1890's small family farm or a 1990's huge high-tech business farm, you'll find out that there's more to the history of farming than ever-improving tractors and bigger cows and pigs.

How long would it have taken to ride a bicycle around an average-sized farm in 1890? Before indoor plumbing, how many miles would a farmer travel back and forth to the outhouse in one year? How is trading baseball cards today like taking produce to market in the old days? Keep turning the pages of *Fun Facts About Farm History* to find out the answers to these questions, and much, much more.

NUMBER OF FARMS

Things sure were different 100 years ago. There were no computers and the cars were powered by steam. There weren't as many people, but there were a lot more farms. You'd think that today, with over three times as many people, we would need more farms. But farms are bigger now, and they can feed more people. Also, there are fewer farms because people don't have to grow their own food. Let's see how today's farms "measure up" to the farms of the past.

CROSS COUNTRY FARMERS

In 1990 there were more than 2 million farms in the U.S. If every one of those farmers stood side by side, that line would stretch from Washington, D.C. to Lincoln, Nebraska. A hundred years earlier there were 4½ million farms. If all those farmers lined up together, they would reach all the way from Washington, D.C. to Los Angeles, California.

FARMS OF PEOPLE

Today there are 5.8 million people living on farms in the United States. That's how many people live in Indiana.

Seem like a lot? In 1900, there were five times that number, or 30 million people, living on farms. That's equal to the number of people who live in California, the most populated state in the country.

REFRIGERATED PIGGY BANKS

Do you keep your coins in a piggy bank? If someone gave you a penny for every farm in the United States today, you would need a piggy bank the size of a refrigerator.

If you had a penny for every one of the 6 million farms in 1942, your giant piggy bank would be the size of three refrigerators!

LESS IS MORE

The number of farms per person in the United States has really decreased in the last 50 years. In 1940, there was one farm for every 22 people. If that many people joined hands, they could make a complete circle around a tractor and hay wagon. Today there is one farm for every 125 people. If all those people joined hands, the amazing ring they could make would circle all the way around an entire barn!

Although there are fewer farms today, they produce 20 times more food than those in 1940.

SIZE OF FARMS

Farmers from 100 years ago would be wide-eyed if they were able to see some of today's farms. Most farms today are over three times bigger than they were at that time. And they can feed many more people, which is a good thing: Since 1900, the number of people in the world has tripled! Farms were able to grow in size because the tractor allowed farmers to plow bigger fields in a shorter amount of time. Let's "size up" these facts about the size of farms.

MEGA FARM

Back in 1910, a farm had an average of 139 acres. If you think that's big, get out your binoculars and take a long look at today's farm. It has an average of 478 acres! You could squeeze almost three-and-a-half farms from 1910 onto one of today's mega-farms.

FARM FLY-BY

A 747 jet is about three-quarters the size of a football field. In 1920, a farmer could have parked 132 of these jumbo jets side by side on a farm.

That's nothing compared to today. Many of today's farms are so big that a farmer could park over 400 of these giant airliners on a farm.

TOUR DE BARNYARD

Want to know how much bigger today's farms are than those from over a hundred years ago? Jump on your bike and start pedaling.

If you can ride your bicycle at 10 miles an hour, it would have taken you 11 minutes to pedal around a farm in 1880. If you decide to cycle around one of today's farms, you'd better bring along a water bottle. This ride would take you longer than 20 minutes.

MILK MADE OF GOLD

Most family farms in the past had a single stall to hold one cow while it was being milked. This provided the family with all the milk they needed in a day. Braum's Dairy in Oklahoma is the largest dairy farm in the world. This massive farm has enough stalls to milk over 12,000 cows.

If all those cows were in their stalls and were lined up side by side, they would make a line as long as seven Golden Gate Bridges in San Francisco, California.

FARM WORK

Have you ever been playing outdoors when you've had to come in because it got too dark? This probably happened to farmers a lot in the past when they ran out of daylight while doing farm work. Without motorized equipment, farmers did all the work by hand or with the help of farm animals. Today's equipment allows a farmer to plow more land and milk more cows each day. Let's take a look back at how farmers got their work done on the farm.

"ACHE-RS" OF WORK

Farm work in the past took more time than you'd think. In 1850, if a farmer wanted to grow an acre of corn, it would have taken a day and a half to plow the field and plant the seeds by hand. With modern equipment, that's enough time for a farmer to plant nearly 300 acres!

GENTLEMEN, START YOUR COWS

No, you're not going to witness a cow-running race at the Daytona 500, but how about a cow-milking race? It might be interesting to watch a milking

contest between a farmer from 1945 and a farmer of today. In 1945 it would have taken a farmer 15 minutes to hand milk a cow. Once machines were invented, cows could be milked at much higher speeds. Today a farmer can milk a cow every 36 seconds!

FOR THE BIRDS

In 1890 it took an entire day to cut enough wheat to make 1,460 loaves of bread. A farmer in 1890 would have been "plowed over" to see a modern

combine on the job. That's because combines cut enough wheat in one day to make 14,000 loaves of bread. You could feed over 1 million more birds with this bread than you could have with the bread from 1890.

HOW DID THEY DO IT?

Harvesting wheat has never been an easy chore to finish, but think of how hard it would have been before the invention of combines. In 1825, it would have taken a farmer nearly a week to cut one acre of wheat by hand, thresh it, and haul it back to the barn for storage.

Farmers today can really cut down on the time it takes, using modern machines like the New Holland TR™ 97 Combine. With this hard-working combine, farmers can harvest up to 75 acres of wheat in one day!

TYPES OF FARMS

In the old days, farms needed to produce enough food for only one family. Most farmers had a variety of crops and animals to provide the food they needed for breakfast, lunch, and supper. Beef and milk came from cows, eggs came from chickens, and flour came from wheat. Those farms were nothing like today's *specialized* farms, which produce only one or two kinds of crops or animals. Let's take a look at just how specialized farms have become.

MUSHROOM MANIA
In the past, mushrooms that grew in the barnyard made a delicious side dish for dinner. Think those farmers had a clue that mushrooms could grow into such a big business? Moonlight Mushrooms uses passageways of an old limestone mine to grow 54 million pounds of mushrooms each year. That's enough to make a mushroom side dish for every person living in the U.S.

JERSEY CITY
At one time, the Jersey cow was just one of several types of cows found on the farm. In 1907, there were 289,000 registered Jerseys

in the U.S. That was enough to give one to each person living in Louisville, Kentucky.

Thanks in part to specialization, today there are nearly 4 million Jersey cows. Now you could give one of those Jerseys to each person living in the entire state of Kentucky!

CHICKEN CONVOY
A few chickens scattered around the barnyard were a part of most family farms of the past. Agrigeneral Co. in Ohio has taken chicken farming to new heights. If the owner decided to move all 5 million chickens, they would need over 10,000 18-wheel trucks to transport all those cluckers.

LET THE COWS DECIDE

Today if you choose to work in the field of agriculture, you would have many choices. You can choose to be a fruit or vegetable grower, a food inspector, or a plant scientist. In the past, if a young person's family raised dairy cows, they usually became dairy farmers. If their family grew wheat or corn, they most likely became crop farmers.

When it came time to decide what they wanted to do in life, you could say it was a decision made "all in the family."

WORKING ANIMALS

Where would farmers have been without animals to help with the farm work in the old days? Probably "up the field without a plow." Animals once pulled a very heavy load on many American farms. A team of horses pulled combines, and cattle helped plow the fields. After the tractor was invented, many animals simply "retired" to the pastures. Animals have helped farmers in many ways, but some are more surprising than others.

HONK IF YOU HEAR ANYTHING

You've probably heard the "woof" of a watchdog or the "ring" of an alarm, but have you ever heard the "honk" of a watchbird? In the 1800's, farmers kept a goose outside the barn at night. It was the goose's job to scare off any unwanted visitors by honking loudly.

DRIVING THEM BUGGY

They weren't exactly hot rods, but horse and buggies were how most farm families traveled before cars were invented. If a family had decided to drive their

horse and buggy from New York City to San Francisco, California, it would have taken them more than a week of non-stop driving. Today, a farm family driving in a car could make the trip in less than two days.

SOME FRIEND YOU ARE

Would you make your best friend operate a machine on a farm? Farmers from the old days often put their dogs on a treadmill that turned a stone wheel which ground wheat into flour.

Those farmers sure got a lot out of "man's best friend"!

HORSING AROUND

The next time you're at a fair or amusement park, check out the carousel. It probably looks similar to when real horses were hitched up to machines on farms. Some farmers used horses to power threshing machines. As the horses walked around in a circle, they turned a gear that made the threshing machine thresh the grain. Did you know that the amount of work that these hard-working animals performed on these machines was the basis for the term "horsepower"?

IMPROVED ANIMALS

Even though animals have gone through changes over time, cows still can't jump over the moon and chickens won't lay golden eggs. Thanks to *genetics*, a method farmers use to change animal characteristics, chickens are laying more eggs and cows are giving more milk. Animals also look a little different than they used to. Now they are even bigger and healthier. Here are some incredible facts about "new and improved" animals.

IMPOSSI-BULL!
It used to be easy to tell one cow from another. Not anymore. In the early 1970's, a man named Art Smith crossed five different cows to produce a new beef cow called the "American Breed." These cows are part Angus, part Hereford, part Brahman, part Charolais, and part Bison. One American Breed bull, named K0-44, weighed 2,750 pounds! That's 750 more lean, mean pounds than the average bull.

WHAT A CHICKEN!
Chickens are laying an average of 17 more eggs a year than they were 20

years ago. Ten chickens now produce 170 more eggs a year than 10 chickens did 20 years ago. You could have an omelette party for 85 people with those "eggs-tra" eggs.

SWIMMING "BULL"
In 1960, one cow produced an average of 1,000 gallons of milk in one year. That sounds like a lot of milk. Through genetics and quality feed, one cow now produces an average of 1,700 gallons of milk.

With that extra 700 gallons of milk, you could fill one big cereal bowl almost 8 feet wide and 2 feet deep.

CITY COOKING

Back in 1820, one farm produced enough food in a day to feed a family of four. Thanks to plant hybrids and animal genetics, plants are yielding more crops per acre and animals are producing more food per day.

A modern farm can now feed over 100 people a day. In one year, a modern farm produces enough food to feed over 36,000 people, or everyone living in Jefferson City, Missouri's capital city, three meals, or a full day's amount of food.

BETTER CROPS

Can you imagine a corn stalk that's higher than a basketball rim? That may sound like a tall tale, but in the 1970's, Dekalb Plant Genetics grew corn that was 14 feet tall! Plants are growing stronger and healthier because of *hybridization*. When a plant is crossed, or hybridized, with another plant of the same family, it improves the plant's quality. Fertilizers help crops grow faster. Together, hybrids and fertilizers add up to bigger and better crops.

'EARS AHEAD

In 1993, United States corn growers actually planted 30 million *fewer* acres of corn than they did in 1930 – an area larger than the size of Ohio. That didn't stop them from harvesting more corn. In fact, if you could hand out all the ears of corn harvested in 1993, you could give almost 25 ears to each person in the U.S. With all the ears from 1930, you could only give seven ears to each person.

JELLY BELLY

A hundred years ago, a farmer usually had a grapevine to make grape jelly or juice. An average farm probably grew enough

grapes to make grape jelly sandwiches for 2,500 people. The largest grape farm, or *vineyard*, in the United States is in Fresno, California. It produces over 6,500 tons of grapes each year. That's enough to make grape jelly sandwiches for more than 500 million people.

COLD CUT ORANGES

Cold weather can harm oranges. Thanks to a new orange hybrid called "Amber Sweet," there may never be another frostbitten orange. Amber Sweets grow faster than the old oranges, which means they can be picked earlier in the season – before Jack Frost can harm them.

SUNFLOWER POWER

Sunflowers are growing taller and taller. In fact, some of these long stem flowers can grow to be over 20 feet tall! You may be surprised to know that some sunflowers are also growing smaller. Michael Lenke of Oregon kept crossing his sunflowers until he created a fully mature sunflower that grew to the unbelievable height of just 2½ inches.

Michael had better watch where he steps when he checks on his crops.

19

FARMHOUSE

Farmhouses have gone through many changes on the American farm. Old farmhouses had wood stoves, hitching posts, and outhouses. Some of today's farmhouses have microwaves, garage-door openers, and swimming pools. Farmers used oil lanterns for light and burned firewood for heat in their log cabins. Today, most farmers use gas or electricity to light and heat their farmhouses. Let's find out just how far the farmhouse has come.

TREE HOUSE

Corn and wheat were primary crops to the farmer in 1850, but trees may have been even more important. Farmhouses were built and heated with wood. And the farmers themselves had to cut down the trees and chop all of the wood. In fact, in order to have enough wood to build a house and heat it for one year, the farmer had to spend up to 45 days cutting trees and chopping wood.

A DIRT HOUSE?

When your mom or dad tells you to clean your room, tell them that your room isn't nearly as "dirty"

as a kind of farmhouse from the past called a *sod house*. It was made out of dirt and grass. If today's farmhouses were covered with sod, you would need more sod than you would find on two little league baseball diamonds to cover one.

OUTHOUSE EXERCISE

Before 1920, many farmhouses didn't have indoor plumbing. That meant a trip to the outhouse was necessary – even on cold winter nights! Some outhouses were as far as 100 feet from the house. With an average of three trips each day, one person would make over 40 miles worth of trips to the outhouse in one year.

HOME ON THE FARM

Outdoor porches have kept a lot of families from "losing their cool." Old farmhouses didn't have air-conditioning, so the family spent much of the summer out on the porch, where the shade kept them cool. Kitchens were also very important. Without any of today's luxuries – electric ovens, food processors, and toasters – most of the meals took a long time to prepare. To cook a roast beef dinner for five people, complete with corn, mashed potatoes, biscuits, and homemade apple pie, it would have taken five hours. Today that dinner would be on the table in about an hour.

FARM PRICES

You can't grow money on farms! That's too bad because farms are expensive to run. A hundred years ago a farmer's main expenses were plant seeds and animal feed. Much of the equipment that is common on today's farms didn't exist at that time. Today's farmer has to buy tractors, milking machines, and special fertilizers. The price farmers charge for their animals and crops has also changed. Here are some facts that make "cents" about farm prices.

ALPHABET FARM

Can you imagine having 26 farms? In 1945, you could buy a farm for $12,000. Today the average farm is worth over $325,000. You could buy 26 farms in 1945 for what you would spend on one farm today.

You could have named each farm starting with a different letter of the alphabet!

THEY'RE WORTH THEIR WOOL

In 1939, there were over 50 million sheep in the United States. There are five times fewer sheep

today. But farmers aren't unhappy, because the price of sheep has gone up ten times. Ten sheep today sell for over $700. A farmer in 1939 had to sell over 100 sheep to make that much money!

Farmers in the old days sure did get more "baaa" for their buck.

MILK MONEY

Could you fit 10 gallons of milk in your refrigerator at home? Your parents probably keep 1 gallon of milk in the refrigerator at any given time.

For what they paid for that one gallon of milk, you could have bought 10 gallons of milk in the early 1900's.

LET'S TRADE

Would you trade a Ken Griffey, Jr., rookie card for a Nolan Ryan card? Trading ball cards today is very similar to how farmers used to buy their goods at the old-style grocery stores. Most farmers brought in butter and eggs and traded them for household items, such as matches, candles, and soap. If today's card-collecting shops took food on trade like the old grocery stores did, you would need to haul in almost 38,000 pounds of butter to buy a 1952 Mickey Mantle baseball card.

STORAGE & DISTRIBUTION

Today food and crops are stored in modern coolers and tanks. Years ago, farms didn't have these convenient storage methods. Farmers used to store milk in 5-gallon cans, and grain was kept in large wooden boxes. When today's food and crops are ready to go to market, they travel in comfort. Milk is taken to a dairy company in large tank trucks, and huge semitrailer trucks take the wheat to a grain mill. Check out the other facts we have "in store" for you.

COOL AS A CUCUMBER

Dogs like to bury things in the yard. Farmers used to bury things too. In the 1800's, in order to keep their vegetables fresh after they were picked, farmers buried them in the ground just beneath the frost line. This "cool" method kept vegetables fresh for several months. Farmers today use refrigerators and freezers to keep their cucumbers, and their other veggies, cool.

START CHOMPING

One way farmers kept their beef fresh was to turn it into beef jerky. This kept the beef fresh for a long time. If you like chewing on beef jerky, you would have been happy on one of these old farms. One 200-pound piece of beef would have kept you chompin' for a whole year!

MILK CAN FALLS

The 5-gallon cans that farmers once stored their milk in are no match for some of today's huge *bulk milk coolers*, which keep the milk cool. It would have taken 1,600 five-gallon cans just to equal one cooler that holds up to 8,000 gallons of milk.

All those cans stacked on top of each other would be almost twice as tall as Yosemite Falls, the highest waterfall in the U.S.

RAILS TO ROADS

In the 1800's, a farmer's main connection to the outside world was the railroad. In order to get their crops to market, farmers loaded them up in a wagon and hauled them by horse to the train station. Trains then transported them to the city. Getting the goods to the train station wasn't an easy job though. Sometimes it would take almost 20 wagon loads just to fill one boxcar. Today, because of paved secondary roads, called market roads, semitrailer trucks that make regular stops at farms can carry most of the cargo to market in one trip.

FARMING SUPERSTITIONS

Can a groundhog's shadow or caterpillar's stripe actually predict the weather? Superstitions – beliefs not based in science that certain actions or events will affect future events – played a major role in farm life of the past. Before radio or TV, farmers had few ways of predicting the weather other than following superstitions and reading <u>The Old Farmer's Almanac</u>. Here are a few superstitions that some farmers have followed for years – and still do.

FROM THE SOUTH SIDE

Some farmers believed that if a north wind blew just before a cow gave birth, the calf would be male. If a south wind blew, it meant the calf would be female. But farmers didn't say what they thought the calf would be if an east or west wind blew.

WEEDING OUT SUPERSTITION

One strange superstition involved a weed called *chess*, a common weed found in many fields. In the early days of farming, some farmers believed that if their wheat was malnour-

ished, or didn't receive the proper care, it would somehow turn into worthless chess.

WEIRD AND WOOLY WEATHER

The "wooly" caterpillars that you can find in the fall are more important than they look. To the superstitious farmer, they are actually miniature weather bugs. Some farmers believe

that a narrow band on the caterpillar means that winter will be very cold. A wide band indicates winter will be warmer than usual.

What a weird and wooly way to wonder about the weather!

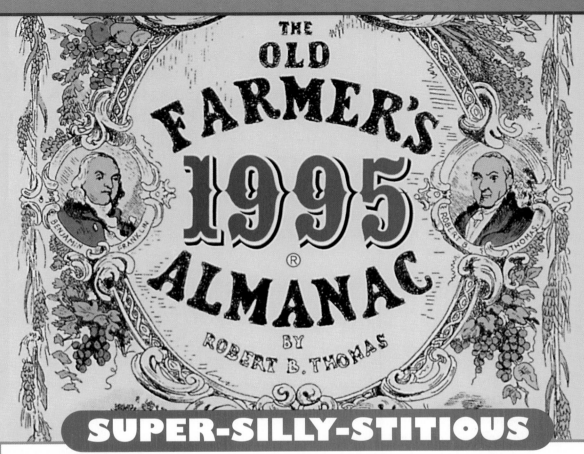

THE OLD FARMER'S 1995 ALMANAC

BY ROBERT B. THOMAS

SUPER-SILLY-STITIOUS

To forecast the weather, or to find out when it is the best possible time to plant their crops, most farmers read <u>The Old Farmer's Almanac</u> by Robert B. Thomas. This famous book has been published every year since 1792, and it is still as popular today as it was over 200 years ago.

Other farmers have followed superstitions. Some believed that if ants traveled in lines, there would be a storm. If the ants scattered, there would be fair weather ahead. Watch for this sign to see if farmers were right about the weather, or if they were just a little "antsy."

FUTURE FARMS

Underwater farms, computerized farms, and space farms. Sound unbelievable? Today with *hydroponics*, crops can be grown in water instead of in soil. Computers are used to feed each cow at dinner on some high-tech farms. And scientists have already proven that food can be grown in space. With increasing technology, there is a good chance that we will see more fascinating farms in the future. Some may even be out of this world!

PIGS IN SPACE
Scientists are interested in raising grains, poultry, and even pigs in space. Just think if we could raise "space pigs." If one-quarter of the total number of pigs today were raised in space, their total weight would be the same as over 2,000 space shuttles.

FISHY FARMERS
Farmers had better take a brush-up course in swimming if they want to run an *aquaculture* farm. Aquaculture is a method of farming fish, shellfish, and seaweeds for food. It was

started in Asia thousands of years ago, but it is now becoming more popular in the United States. Instead of checking the temperature of a bulk milk cooler, farmers may one day be checking the saltiness of their seawater crops.

LAPTOP COWS?
To increase milk production, some dairy farmers are already using computers to give each cow a precise amount of food and vitamins. One farm in Churchville, New York, increased its milk production from 19,000 pounds in a year to nearly 21,000 pounds by using computers. That's an extra 250 gallons of milk per year!

PLANT SCIENCE

Growing plants in a scientific laboratory, or even underwater, seems unbelievable compared to planting them in soil. Using a technique called hydroponics, scientists grow plants inside large trays of water. While the plants are suspended in water, their roots absorb water and minerals for nourishment.

Farmers in the past walked through their fields to check the growth of their crops. Farmers in the year 2095 may have to swim through them.

DAYS GONE BY

Now you have seen how, throughout history, farms have played a very important role in our lives, and still do. For many years, farming was a way of life for most American families. Fields were plowed with the help of horses, and cows were milked by hand. Today, most farms are specialized big businesses that use high-powered milking machines, air-conditioned tractors, and huge combines to get the work done.

We hope that *Fun Facts About Farm History* has shown you how fascinating the history of farming can be. You'll never look at farm history the same way again!

SAFETY TIPS

A farm is a wonderful place to live and visit, but it isn't always safe. In the old days, tractors and other equipment were unshielded and farmers ran the risk of being hurt. Today machinery has shields to protect farmers from moving parts. Even though farms are much safer than they once were, they can still be very dangerous. Here are some smart safety tips to keep in mind while on the farm.

1. Prepare for emergencies. Post telephone numbers and directions to the farm next to all phones. Always keep a first aid kit nearby, such as in the barn and in the tractor cabs. Encourage family members to take a course in CPR and first aid.

2. Tractors are not toys. They have an important job to do. Though it may look like fun, do not ride on tractors. There have been many incidents where extra riders have been hurt or even killed after falling off a tractor, even a tractor with a cab.

3. Never play in or on grain. Equipment that is used to transport and store grain on the farm have hidden dangers. Grain flowing from bins, wagons, or trucks can pull you under and lead to suffocation.

4. Stay away from moving parts on machinery, especially chains, belts, and PTO's. Shields on PTO's, augers, and other farm machinery should be secure.

Because farm life involves being outdoors and around equipment, sometimes a farm can seem like a large playground. But living and working on a farm has many hazards. Farm Safety 4 Just Kids works to prevent farm-related childhood injuries, health risks, and fatalities. Contact the organization at 1-800-423-KIDS to learn more about staying safe on the farm. A healthy and safe farm is a happy farm, so always stay alert.

Order The Replica

Whether you are a serious collector or just a big fan of farm toys, you should consider a subscription to The Replica. This 4-color, bi-monthly magazine comes to you direct from The Ertl Company. It's full of the latest news about upcoming product releases in die cast farm toys, farm playsets, banks and other Ertl collectibles. And, from time to time, special subscriber-only, exclusive products are offered.

To receive your subscription of The Replica, write to:

The Ertl Company Replica Offer
Dept. 776A Highways 136 & 20
P.O. Box 500, Dyersville, IA 52040-0500

Inside the U.S.A. $10.00 for 1 year and $18.00 for 2 years
Outside the U.S.A. $14.00 for 1 year and $22.00 for 2 years

Farm Safety ♥ Just Kids

For more information on how to stay safe on the farm, call or write:

Farm Safety 4 Just Kids
110 South Chestnut Avenue
P.O. Box 458
Earlham, IA 50072

1-800-423-KIDS or 1-515-758-2827

Fun Facts About Farm History was created in cooperation with Farm Safety 4 Just Kids.